In the name of God, infinitely mercifull, eternally compassionate

DEAD SEA SCROLL WITH BLESSINGS FROM EARLY KORAN & BUDDHA

For Bawa, who was truth

made visible,
who shared his love secrets.
Who taught us
Separate from yourself
that which separates you from others.

VISIT ONE SONG ONLINE AT
WWW.THEILLUMINATIONCO.COM
MOST OF THE ART IN THIS BOOK IS AVAILABLE
AS PRINTS, POSTERS AND CARDS.

RUNNING PRESS
PHILADELPHIA • LONDON

Come!

Let us choose one another as Companions.
Let us sit at one another's feet.

Come a little closer now,
so that we may see each other's faces.

Inside we share so many secrets~
Do not believe we are simply what these eyes can see.

Now we are music together,
sharing one cup and an armfull of roses.

This blurry mandala-pattern is actually the first photographic image ever made of DNA–the work of a Rosalind Franklin. From it, Watson and Crick deduced the DNA double helix shape, and eventually *how life propagates itself*. The images in this book arise from like purpose: art not as personal expression but as a collaborative search for fresh insight into the mystery of human existence. Finding such imagry is a process that builds on the richness of what has gone before. My deep appreciation, then, to the mostly anonymous artists whose work informs these illuminations. And to all those who helped this book and music come into being. Thanks to Coleman for the use of his Rumi renditions herein (a few songs lean on his work as well). To Saliha, who didn't interfere and left nothing undone; to musicians David Mowry, Jeff Sheard and Kabir ...and Jerry Foreman, Amira Dvorah, Clare Maher, Muhammad Sultan, Shams Kairys, Gene Sheilds, Dale Melton, Bill Zinno & Kevin Delany, too. To Jamey Reilly and Bill Taylor for their Psalms; to Shakina Reinhertz for a good turn; to Michaela Majoun for encouragement; to Gary Elliot for being an evangelist; to Matthew & Joan for *not* being; to Craig Johnson for his ever-readiness to help; to Annie Dillard, Andrew Harvey, Lew Welsh and Ken Wilber for quotes; to David Federman for poetic inspiration; to Jonathan Granoff for standing guard; to Snatum Kaur & Thomas Barquee for music that let me weep; to Reid Boates for marketplace clarity; to editor Deborah Grandinetti for letting things flower; to publisher John Whalen who saw that some books should sing; and to Kitty Kallen– help beyond price.

If these poems repeat themselves...

then so does Spring.

CONTENTS
CHAPTERS   SONGS

INTRODUCTION

Somewhere in thirteenth century Persia, a famous mystical poet meets a precocious boy not yet in his teens and recognizes something brilliant. *Someday your words will be heard around the world,* he says. The poet was Attar, the boy Jelaluddin Rumi, and 700 years later that prophesy is coming true. Already vastly popular in the Islamic world, Rumi is now America's most-read poet. In these weird and wicked days, his words are building a bridge of love over one of the great divides of our time.

It's been said that for those who believe in God no explanation is needed; and for those who don't, none is possible. There's a similar divide between the Believers who are certain their God is the only God, and those who are equally confident that a God of Infinite Mercy would be present in all great faiths. This is a deep ravine, but there are possibilities of bridge-building. Some years ago, the governing council of the fellowship I belong to was mired in debate over some minor issue. People dug in; there was no give. Then Ajwad, our eldest, joined us. Ajwad had just recovered from six months of total blindness, and the ordeal lent him a quiet gravity. He listened and spoke. Nothing extraordinary, but everyone became still. He was coming from a deeper place than us, and we all heard it. The conflict evaporated. Rumi is like that: his current runs deeper than words.

He is both devout Muslim, and a faithful witness to a grace abounding beyond all doctrines. *Rumi reminds us,* says poet Coleman Barks, *of the radiant depth inside that is present in grief and in love, in being ecstatically here in the moment. What he celebrates has many names—the soul, Buddha nature, the person of Christ, the Nur, and Rumi praises them all at one table. There is no quarrel about names or scriptures in Rumi. His work does not divide; it includes, and that is a blessing in these sectarian days. Rumi represents a nourishing exchange for both the East and the West, like the Silk Road was in his day, where the beauties of the great religions and the storytellers and poets and their music flowed together and mixed into a new and vibrant fusion.*

Rumi's popularity today can be largely attributed to the poetic ministry of Coleman. He comes to the task with a southern preacher's ease with words, a generous heart, and a humbling connection with the same Sufi Master I sat with, Bawa Muhaiyaddeen. Coleman has kindly let me use a number of his renditions herein which I will identify with his totem Maypop flower: ❀ The rest are my interpretations, and I happily confess my debt to Arberry, Nicholson, Barks, and the other Rumi-miners. If family resemblances appear, they honor the flowing source we all drew from—just as the great prophetic streams of Judaism, Christianity, and Islam all praise the singular God of Abraham. All one family, all one song.

It's tempting to look for connections between our age and Rumi's. Like us, he found himself in a world dissolving at the edges. In his time, it was the Persian Empire, a vast and aging imperium increasingly unable to defend itself. Mongol barbarians had begun swooping out of the steppes to pillage a town or city. One can imagine rumors of atrocities sweeping through a hundred marketplaces, a whole population with the jitters. As a child, Rumi lived near the vulnerable frontier metropolis of Balkh–now in Afghanistan. One day his father packed up his family and headed west in search of safer lands. Traveling the ancient Silk Road they finally settled on the western rim of the empire in the town of Konya, today in western Turkey.

By the time he was thirty, Jelaluddin was deeply versed in the mystical lore of the Sufis, and the leader of a spiritual community brought together by his father. All this was ended abrupt-ly by an encounter in the Konya marketplace with a wandering, rough-hewn master named Shams of Tabriz. Shams means "the Sun," and he was by all evidence an extraordinarily awakened soul.

Accounts of the meeting differ. One has Shams pitching all of Rumi's literary works into a fountain, Rumi objecting, and Shams pulling the books out dry and undamaged. Whatever happened, Rumi suddenly, overwhelmingly knew he was in the presence of authentic, dizzying divinity. *Everything that I have studied and talked about I have met in a person*, he said. Abandoning home, students, status, and friends, Rumi vanished into the desert with Shams. We will never know what manner of spiritual work filled their retreats, but it threw Rumi far beyond the boundaries of conventional religion. A great soul-fire was ignited, and we still feel its radiance 700 years later.

Seek pearls from an oyster,
skills from a craftsman.
And if you find someone ripe
in wisdom, don't go away
empty-handed.

Mastering a craft calls for practice;
spiritual quickening
needs intimate companionship
with a true teacher.

Deep in the heart
every mystery of spirit
is hidden.
Only from Soul can soul draw

its secrets, not
from any page or eloquent speech.
The heart of the matter is soul,
Nothing else.
Nothing you can ever hear,
ever do.

Sufi master M.R. Bawa Muhaiyaddeen

THE ILLUMINATION BAND

DAVID MOWRY, JEFF SHEARD & KABIR GREEN

LIVE!

RUMI'S POEMS
AS FOUND IN VARIOUS
SONGS, CHANTS &
METAPHYSICAL FIELD HOLLERS

WWW.THEILLUMINATIONBAND.COM

This music business started easily enough. Coleman needed accompaniment at an upcoming concert reading, so I got together with guitarist David Mowry one weekend to work up some music. Afterward, David started idly noodling around, and I heard something evocative. *Can you play Appalachian music?* David went right to some old plaintive air. I flipped open THE ILLUMINATED RUMI to a random poem. *Sing this?* First hesitant, David quickly found the range, and a thirteenth century Persian poem suddenly morphed into an old mountain lament. Two rivers of longing merged with hardly a ripple. We both knew we had found something. I started rhyming free verse into song lyrics, and together with drummer Jeff Sheard and my son Kabir, we began shaping some Rumi ballads. Style wandered through primitive blues, gospel, and country music that would be at home in a West-Texas truck stop. And why not? Rumi evokes a sacredness where culture differences slip away, and a homegrown bluegrass mysticism feels just about right. The group received a standing ovation that first night, and have been playing ever since. It's a well-worn path. For seven centuries, musicians across the Middle East and India have been singing Rumi, each in their own tradition. THE ILLUMINATION BAND has joined this communion. In fairness, these songs are yet another layer of interpretation, and they should be billed as *from* Rumi. As with the poetry renderings here, if just a taste of his original intention seeps through, that's nourishment enough.

• Bawa used to talk about a mighty tree that once grew in the east, died, and fell to the west. *But its seeds*, he said, *were taking root in new soil.* •

Y ou've heard how Moses
was with God on Sinai. That

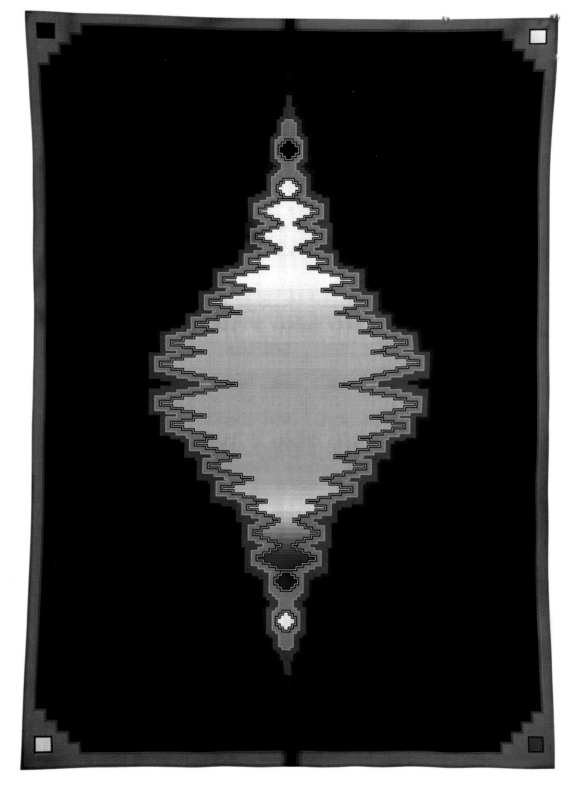

closeness is far away now. Look
at the overcast sky: it's not

the splendor of feeling near.
We've been lazy. We should

either disband altogether or
not stay apart so long. Let

music loosen our deafness
to spirit. Play and let play.

O Amazing Love

O AMAZING LOVE,
LET ME SING OF YOUR WONDERS
WITH THESE WORDS
LET ME OPEN
A DOOR
INTO LIGHT

At one time or another, I believe everyone gets the Call. The shutters open for an instant and perfection tumbles through. Maybe it is a rainy day, and you are eleven years old, watching a drop of water slowly slide down the windowpane–into eternity. Or maybe one sunrise, losing yourself you become a flight of birds. But after the Call there's a whole lot of forgetting. Or, if not forgetting, a reluctance to accept its full consequences, which is to become obsessed with regaining your true identity. Rumi says the only thing that can drive this great quest is a *special kind of love.* It's not infatuation or sensual excitement, though these agitations sometimes work as coming attractions. This love, this oceanic love, is really dangerous: one sip can send you spinning forever. Rumi is a change-agent, and he wants nothing more than to shake us to the roots and turn us around forever. Can we trust this man as a spiritual friend? Real trust doesn't arise from persuasive arguments, but it might from a taste of Amazing Love. There's more than a taste around Rumi; there's a flowing heart-river. *Faith, hope, and love,* the Bible says, *these three, but the foremost is love.* I would follow him anywhere. If we can stand for even one moment on the shore of his heart, we may catch a small glimpse of what he sees and how he knows things. Implicit in all these poems, these love poems, is his poignant invitation: *Will you join me?* All the heavens will be decorated, and all the angels will sing, on the day his call and our response become one and the same song.

If you can't wrap this love
around you like a cloak at midnight,
don't put on something else,
       go back to bed.

Let THIS LOVE run spinning
through your brain.
It's what holds everything together,
    and it's the everything too!

Without a little dancing,
there is no disappearing.

LOVE SO VAST,
LOVE THE SKY CANNOT CONTAIN.
HOW DOES ALL THIS FIT INSIDE MY HEART?

Whoa! In this mob of *I's* inside,

which one is *me?*

Hear me out.

I know I'm wandering, but

don't start putting a lid on this racket.

No telling what I'll do then.

Every moment I'm thrown by

your story. One moment it's happy, and

I'm singing. One moment it's sad, and

I'm weeping. It turns bitter, and

I pull away.

But then you spill a little grace, and just like that,

I'm all light.

It's not so bad,

this arrangement,

actually.

Good, old-time monotheism has managed to churn up some pretty heavy-handed versions of Yahweh in its day. When God the Dominator glowers down from some Byzantine church, better dive for cover. Not much love radiating there. But with Rumi we're privy to real contact with sacredness, and the living presence is quite different. Fear-based boundaries and mental certainties dissolve when mystical love starts flowing. Ramakrishna (the Hindu saint who embraced Christianity and then Islam just to see if GOD, ALLAH, and TRUTH-CONSCIOUSNESS-BLISS were identical*) used to say that this contact was like "a salt doll exploring the sea." Dispatches from such a front are bound to be a little diffused, as we see in the shape-shifting, divine *You* that Rumi is always addressing. Sometimes *You* is a stupendous overarching Divine Presence. Then it is the intimacy of the Friend, as when he experiences that vastness through the person of Shams. Sometimes *You* is a Beloved, all feminine and alluring, and Rumi is whispering *I would love to kiss You.* Altogether, it's a charged, slightly scandalous situation, and his genius is to make us accomplices, guilty as charged.

Diving into the ocean deeps, or waving *this way* from the shore, there's a big secret Rumi has to pass on: *At some point, the salt doll becomes the sea.* When the smoke-and-mirrors ego surrenders to Vastness, there's nothing left but *holy holy holy,* and ecstatic, total identification with Godhead. This is over the edge for most folk, something to put off to the Rapture. But we still want Rumi to tell us, again and again, *holy holy is what you really are,* right now. He liked to invoke the legendary Hallaj, a Sufi who was constantly drawn into union, then unable to stop himself from exclaiming inside the streaming galactic whirl, "I am Light! I am Truth!"

*He concluded they were.

12

Last night I took a vow, by your life this time,
that I would never again turn my eyes from your face.
Pierce me with a sword, I will not look away from you.

Cast me into a fire, I won't even sigh.
You pass, and I rise from your path like dust.
Now, like dust, I settle back to earth.

COME!
JUST LISTEN.

We know a way from
your scene
to the Unseen. You've

lived too long in that
gloomy house. This
path leads to a garden

that will lift you
right out of yourself.
The gardener is an

old friend, the cypress
and jasmine too.
Every day

we come and gather
a hundred blossoms
here to scatter

among you.
Don't worry, there are
no hidden motives,

just too much
love blooming
to keep for ourselves.

These words
are a fragrance escaping
from this garden. See

how the world
is softened by their
sweetness. Hear

them whisper,
*Come! Come! It
really is like this!*

When we first caught
the scent, it
swept us away, then

gave us greatness.
And even if we are
nothing more than

servants of love now,
take care! **Like love,
we wait in ambush.**

HAS ANYONE BEEN SWEPT UP IN THIS WAVE
AND NOT MOVED TO THE BEACH?
WAS THERE EVER A FISH THAT FLED FROM THE SEA,
OR A CANVAS THAT TURNED FROM THE BRUSH?

ALONE, I'M A NAME WITH NO MEANING,
BUT THIS LOVING IS SO CHARGED WITH
MEANING IT DOESN'T NEED NAMES!
STILL, LET'S SAY IT ALL AGAIN:

YOU'RE THAT SEA, I'M THAT FISH, AND IT'S ALL
YOUR SHOW: MELTING HEART OR IMPERIAL DECREE,
I'LL TAKE EVERYTHING. BUT WHAT
KIND OF LOVE IS THIS? YOU SLIP AWAY

FOR A SINGLE MOMENT, AND THE WHOLE WORLD
BURSTS INTO FLAME. YOU RETURN, AND
ALL THAT FIRE SLIPS BACK INTO THE CANDLE
THAT LIGHTS UP MY CHEST.

IF SOMEONE ASKS,
"WHAT KIND OF LOVE IS THIS?" SAY,
LET GO YOUR TILLER AND SEE! THOSE
WHO HAVEN'T ABANDONED FREE WILL
　　WILL NEVER KNOW.

DIVE INTO THIS LOVE
AND THE WORLD PARTS BEFORE YOU.
THIS LOVE AND YOU ARE
CIRCLING OUTSIDE OF TIME.
　　EVERYTHING ELSE

IS BORROWED AND CRUMBLING.
WHAT IS BORN IN THE SPRING FADES
IN THE FALL. DON'T PINE FOR A
BEAUTIFUL CORPSE. THIS LOVE
　　IS THE ROSE

　　　　THAT

BLOOMS FOREVER.

WHEN **THIS KIND OF LOVE** FINALLY

MELTS THE HEART

THERE'S
NO SHORTAGE OF
CRITICS AND USELESS ADVICE!

DOGS BARK AT THE MOON & WHAT'S THE HARM?

THIS KIND OF LOVE

MAKES YOU A MOUNTAIN, NOT SOME FLUFF IN THE WIND.

There's blame.
a rule some- Cultivate this
where that **This** garden, and
Kind of Love everywhere
gathers blame, else is going
another that it turns to seem like
a deaf ear to desolation row.

"Welcome!"

JESUS CALLS

"Come wash at the fountains,
Come sit at the table."

• IT'S THE TAVERN OF ANIHILATION !

GO AHEAD. YOU'VE SPENT TOO MUCH TIME ALREADY, CALL-
ING FOR JUSTICE IN THE DECEIVER'S COURTHOUSE.
JUST GET TO THAT TABLE. THERE'S A DRINK WAIT-
ING THERE THAT WILL STILL ALL YOUR JUSTICE
CHATTER. AFTER ALL, YOU'RE A LOVER,
AND
THIS KIND OF LOVE
IS

BEST SIPPED IN SILENCE

fig. 1

ARE YOU SHADOW IN LOVE WITH THE SUN? LET THE SUN COME!

• WARNING •
With this love, bitterness becomes honey • With this love, copper becomes gold • With this love, dregs become wine • With this love, pain becomes a healing herb • With this love, death becomes life • With this love, the king becomes a slave.

fig. 2

THE REED SONG

For Rumi, the beauty of *union* is tied to the longing for it. The plaintive music of the reed flute reflects its yearning to return to its original home in the riverbank. This is the opening poem in his great work the *Mathnavi*, and by happy coincidence, the first we put to song.

Listen to a simple story
Told by a reed taken from its home.
Here's a tale for all you people
Who've wandered lost and all alone.

Since I was cut from out the reed-bed
I have made this crying sound.
Anyone parted from a true love
Knows the sorrow that I have found.

Anyone pulled from Source and center
And taken far from house and home
longs to return to where the roots are,
longs to rest, no more to roam.

Now if you gather I too will be there,
In the laughter and the grief,
A friend to one and to the other
Above, behind, before, beneath.

But few will hear the deepest secrets
hidden in my trembling air.
There are no ears can hear these secrets,
Only a heart that's stripped and bare.

Body flows from out of Spirit.
Spirit flows from out our form.
We can't conceal that mystic mixing,
Nor see the soul when it's never been born.

This flute is filled with God's own fire,
No earthly wind can play its tune.
Just be that empty, and be that hollow,
Reflect the light like the full moon.

Hear the love-fire full of yearning
Tangled with each note in space,
As bewilderment and my heart's sorrow
Turns into wine of amazing grace.

The reed is friend to every pilgrim
Who prays the veil be torn away.
The reed is hurt and salve combining.
Darkest night and brightest day.

Intimacy, and the longing for it,
A single song they have become.
A disastrous, complete surrender,
And finest love, becoming one.

There are hundreds of ways joy can find us, and numberless individuals have followed the path of joy into the luminous dissolving realm of Amazing Love. But the way is subtle and runs against the current of ordinary achievement. Guides are needed, and guides there are, says Rumi. Some are around us as invisible mirrors, but always, in plain view, are those who came as soul-teachers to the ages. Sufis call these shining stars *Nabis*, a word usually translated as *prophet*, although this usage does little justice to the full meaning. We usually envision prophets as lonely oracles graced (or sometimes crazed) with flashes of divine foresight. The Nabi is of an entirely different order. The Nabi is fully immersed in the Beloved and brings such loving vastness of spirit as to awaken the higher angels of a people, or a planet. In the teachings of the Sufis, "A Nabi is sent to *every* people."

> *The Noble One said,*
> *"I am an ark in the swift flood of time, and my companions, a fellowship.*
> *Who throws in with us sails into light."*

> *With this kind of master, all meanness stays on shore. He's*
> *a soul-saver. Under his gaze you'll sail safely even in sleep.*
> *To every time such a captain is sent, so hold fast*
> *to his hand, and beware your own strengths.*
> *Without a guide, even the noble-hearted can get filled with themselves.*

There's something enormous about the prophetic incarnation. A child is born, supernovas flair. He cries, and dried-up breasts overflow with milk. A few words are spoken, and empires collapse. Rumi hints at this scale in an anecdote: A distraught mother runs to Ali, Muhammad's son-in-law. Her baby has somehow gotten out to the edge of a roof where she cannot go and is ignoring her entreaties to return to safety. *Bring another baby up to the roof*, says Ali. She does, and her child, seeing a companion, crawls away from danger. Rumi continues,

> *The Nabis come in human form for this reason, that we may see them*
> *as familiars, delight in their friendship,*
> *and crawl away from the edges of roofs.*

Come in *human form*? As opposed to what? When the Incarnation declares *I am the Way and the Truth and the Light, and only through me may you enter the Kingdom*, who or what is speaking? Is it a particular individual, a regional appearance like us? Or is it the infinite *I Am that I Am* which can speak from human tongue, or whirlwind, or burning bush, or howsoever It wishes? If we project an ordinary level of comprehension into these words, we may be cutting ourselves off from the connecting strength of the mighty prophetic family—and dooming ourselves to feel superior to whole portions of the human family.

What if a Lightbringer was sent to every nation? There is a such a generous ring of truth to the notion! If it meets resistance in us, or grates against some idea dearly held, we might try to search our psyche for some part that *needs others to be wrong for us to be right, or special or saved*. Is it vanity? Perhaps humility could be useful here. I remember a helpful bumper sticker: *May the baby Jesus open our minds and shut our mouths.*

HOW THEY SHINE, THIS GRAND PROCESSION,
THIS PRICELESS GIFT, THIS
SHINING CHAIN OF GOLD.

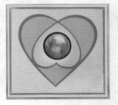

TURN AWAY FROM ONE, YOU TURN
FROM ALL THE REST. LOOK,
EACH A SPLASH OF BRIGHT SUNLIGHT.
ONE SUN, SEEN
THROUGH DIFFERENT WINDOWS.

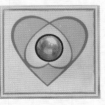

Harmonic convergence: Jews, Christians, Muslims, Hindus and Buddhists all look eagerly to the coming of a *Messiah*. Both Christians and Muslims identify him as *Jesus*, Hindus call him *Kalki*, and Buddhists, *Maitreya*. I leave you, dear Reader, to draw your own conclusion.

OMETHING BIG
IS COMING.
IT'S STILL SECRET, BUT
ARRIVING EVERYWHERE.
THE PILGRIMS AND THE
MYSTERY–LOVERS KNOW.
THEY'RE GATHERING NOW,
SHY, HEART-SHAPED, PINK-CHEEKED,
WANDERING IN FROM THE GARDEN.
SEE HOW THOSE WHO HAVE SIPPED THE
MILK OF GENEROSITY ARE
SO ALIVE TO WHERE IT'S COMING FROM NEXT.
THE ATMOSPHERE IS CHARGED
WITH LONGING AND SEARCHING.
THEN THE SOUND OF PRAYER DRIFTS
ACROSS THE DAWN. IT'S MUSLIM,
JEW, AND CHRISTIAN
ALL MINGLED...

When hearts harden, the lines in the sand get deeper, and the need to affirm the unity of the prophets becomes more pressing. But the truth will be found in soul-work, not archeological digs into the past. Driving with Bawa, my friend Jonathan Granoff once wondered why all the prophets came from deserts in the Middle East. Bawa answered with unexpected fierceness: *I did not come here to teach history!* The point was clear. Better to approach the prophets as stations outside of time, present and available as internal substance. Jesus points to his heart because that's where he is—*in your heart*. And it's where you are—*in his heart*. The Nabi-prophet has plunged into the sea of Friendship and become a great ocean current able to carry whole flotillas. This Grace Stream is not the work of some historical figure, nor the directive of a supernatural being looking *down* on us, but an active strength and beauty *inside*.

ALL RELIGIONS, ALL THIS SINGING,
ONE SONG.
THE DIFFERENCES ARE JUST
ILLUSION AND VANITY.
THE SUN'S LIGHT LOOKS
A LITTLE DIFFERENT ON THIS WALL THAN
IT DOES ON THAT WALL,
AND A LOT DIFFERENT ON THIS OTHER ONE,
BUT IT'S STILL ONE LIGHT.

WE HAVE BORROWED THESE CLOTHES,
THESE TIME AND PLACE PERSONALITIES
FROM A LIGHT,
AND WHEN WE PRAISE,
WE'RE POURING THEM BACK IN.

A HUNDRED SUNS
FILL A HUNDRED COURTYARDS
UNTIL ALL THE WALLS COME DOWN.

T HERE'S A DOOR OF GREAT MYSTERY;
SINGLE AND UNCHANGING,
BUT THE DOORKEEPERS ARE MANY.
ONE BY ONE, THEY COME AND SERVE.

HERE'S AN OLD DOORKEEPER SECRET:
WHAT ONE DOES IS THE DEED OF ALL.
KING DAVID CAN RAISE UP A TEMPLE
WITH SOLOMON'S HANDS.

ALL THE DOODKEEPERS,
JUST SO MANY CURTAINS
OVER ONE GREAT LION SOUL.

ANOTHER KIND OF SOUL ANIMATES OUR BODIES.
IT ROAMS THE WORLD OF SEPARATIONS,
A LAND WHERE THE BIG WOLF EATS,
AND THE REST GO HUNGRY,
WHERE A WEAK WOLF DIES,
AND THE PACK REJOICES.

ONE LION, MANY WOLVES.

The Noble Prophet said: *May divine light rise before me, behind me, to the right and left, above and below.*
May my limbs be filled with divine light. May my skin be filled with divine light.

I called through your door,
"The mystics are gathering
in the streets. Come out!"

"Leave me alone.
I'm sick."

"I don't care if you're dead!
Jesus is here, and he wants
to resurrect somebody!"

A Great Wedding

is being celebrated in the
Golden Kingdom

Such feasting! Such joy!
Such splendor in every particle!

No need to inquire
if your heart's not on fire.

...but down in the unlit places,
the poor didn't even raise their eyes.
So messengers were sent
in every direction with invitations

numberless as stars.

In the Sufi understanding there are 124,000
Nabis, known and unknown, but a few bear
a special fullness. Their names and gifts are
a litany that gathers humanity together.
Among them...

ABRAHAM IS THE FRIEND OF GOD
MOSES IS THE WORD OF GOD
JESUS IS THE SOUL OF GOD
MUHAMMAD IS THE MESSENGER OF GOD

COME FOR THE BEST OF DAYS, FOR A FESTIVAL
OF ROSES, FOR WHAT ONLY GETS BETTER.

COME RAISE A JOYFUL NOISE,
FOR WE HAVE DISCOVERED THE
FRIEND, BELOVED,
AND GUIDE.

WHAT ELSE IS THERE IN
THE WORLD LIKE THIS? THIS
IS DELICIOUSNESS
SPILLING

EVERYWHERE AND THE ROAR OF
INVISIBLE OCEANS, THE WORLD
GONE WAVY. THIS IS
JESUS

ARRIVING FROM HIS HEAVENS,
MUHAMMAD RETURNING
FROM HIS LIFT INTO
LIGHT.

Our Father's overflowing
grace, and the radiant light
which emerged within it
became a fruit that oozed
into radiant Mary. It became
a jewel for the world. It
appeared at the beginning
of creation and became the life
within all lives
in the eternal world.

It appeared in the beginning
of creation and existed as a realm
in the Universe of the Soul.
It became the treasure, the soul,
It became the treasure, the soul.
Finally it became the symbolic form
of Jesus, it became
the symbol of Jesus.

—*Bawa Muhaiyaddeen,*
May God be ever pleased with him

HOW USELESS THE COIN NOT MINTED HERE! HOW
TASTELESS THE WINE NOT POURED FROM THIS CUP!

In Sufi tradition there are light-beings known as *Qutbs* who are ever appearing to renew the truth of the prophetic revelation. Rumi by all appearences was one, and in modern times, our Bawa Muhaiyaddeen. The atmosphere around such a one is subject to extraordinary weather changes. Like Rumi, Bawa's attention would often shift unexpectedly to another dimension. Rumi might start reciting poetry; Bawa would begin to sing. Praise or prayer or conversation, who knew? For us it was standing in the pure rain of grace. Above are a few words from one such spontaneous song. There's such extraordinary warmth in the way it embraces Mary and Jesus. Sufis like to invoke the blessings of God upon a Lightbringer whenever mentioning his or her name. It's a recognition that their true and living form is abiding *inside us in a secret place,* and by pausing to offer greetings we are awakening an eternal connection. The reader is invited to do so as he reads.

Mother & Child by Adolphe Bouguereau, Center of Galaxy by Hubble

What's
the use of prayer
or religion when the
Soul of the soul is here?
What good is the soul now,
but for giving away?
I was empty, his love made me a mountain.
I was a mountain, it made me a handful
of straw. Where does he come from?
Where? I'm giving up,
just let me sit near this love,
as breath is near body.
Friends and companions,
lay down your load.

When
Solomon
approaches the throne,
all darkness retreats. Why hesitate?
Even if you haven't a thing to say, find
your way to the hall.
Run, bring your prayers and your problems,
your secret desires. Come, the king
knows the hidden meanings
of every language, speaks even
birdtalk. It's all just wind anyway, our
speech before Solomon.
Come just to hear
his command:

"GATHER TOGETHER THE ONES WHO ARE SCATTERED."

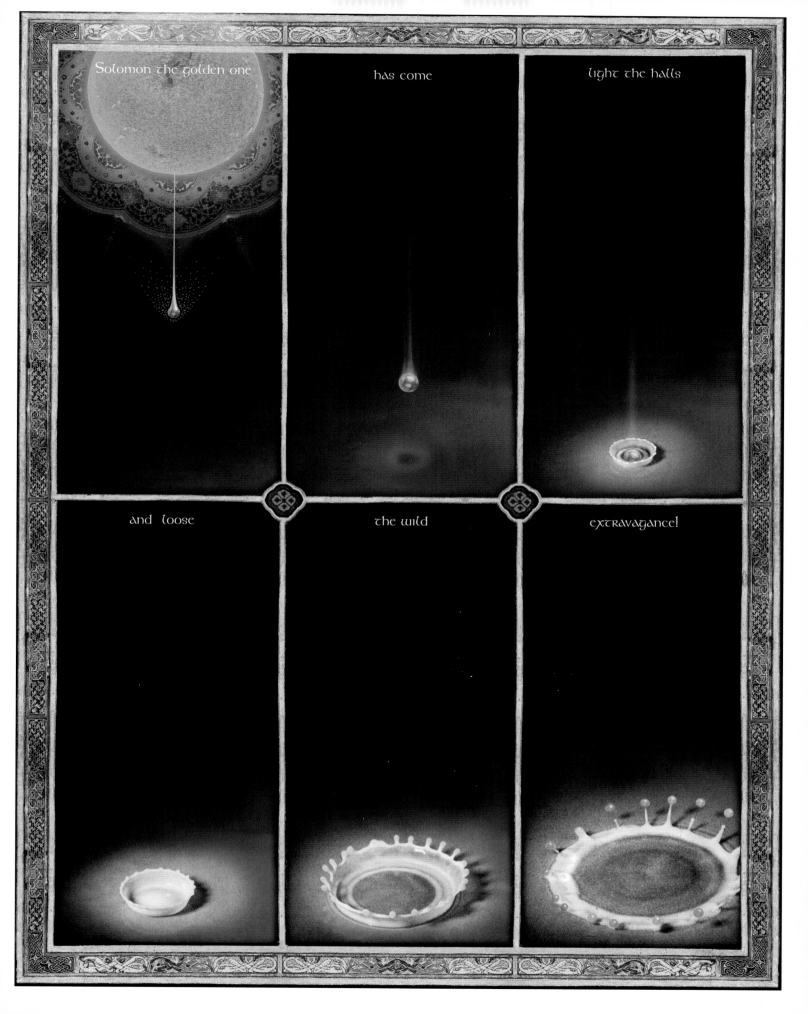

WHEN MOSES APPROACHED
THE BURNING BUSH, IT SPOKE SAYING,

COME, I AM
THE HEALING WATERS.

PUT OFF YOUR SHOES, FOR
YOU STAND ON SACRED GROUND.

AND DO NOT FEAR,
I AM COOLING, SOFT AND SWEET.

TODAY I SPREAD A SEAT OF HONOR,
AND THE SEAT IS YOURS.

HIGH IN HEAVEN IS A PEARL,
AND THE PEARL IS YOU.

DEEP IN THE EARTH IS A RUBY,
AGAIN IT IS YOU.

WHEREVER YOU STAND, YOU SHALL
BE THE SOUL OF THAT PLACE.

AND YOU SHALL ALSO BE THE EMPTINESS
WHEREIN ALL PLACES FIND REST.

YOUR BRIGHT GAZE WILL KINDLE
THIS OLD SHADOW WORLD TO

BLAZE UP ONCE AGAIN
WITH THE FIRE OF FAITH.

WHEREVER
YOU STAND
BE THE SOUL
OF THAT PLACE.

In his youth, Moses tended
sheep, and he was a careful
herdsman. Once, one
of his lambs strayed into
the wilderness, and he left
the rest and followed its trail
till his feet were blistered,
and his sandals all torn.

At last, as day turned to night,
he found the creature
spent and afraid,
and he gathered it up
into his arms, and stroked
its back, and brushed the dust
from its fleece, and comforted it
like a mother, saying,

> *My poor thing, what*
> *troubles you have brought me...*
> *but why be so cruel to yourself?*

And upon his face not a line
of irritation, nothing
but love, and pity, and tears.
Then the Creator of all things
spoke to the angels, saying
> *This one is the stuff of prophethood.*

The noble Muhammad has said,
> *Every prophet is a shepherd*
> *once, for God would not*
> *bestow His mantle on one unschooled*
> *in hardship. A long while*
> *I was a shepherd that I might gather*
> *calmness and fortitude.*

It's wonderful how present the prophets are in Rumi's conversation. Joseph or Noah or Moses appear in the same familiar way that legendary uncles and aunts enter into dinner conversations at Thanksgiving. It's the same living relationship that you see in medieval manuscripts depicting Mary and Joseph as European peasants. I don't know where some of Rumi's accounts came from, if they are traditional folktales, gospel accounts that slipped the Judeo-Christian net—or revelation. What I see is how much the prophets are *family* in Rumi's world. That's a gift. Bawa was on the same first-name standing with the Lightbringers, and he made it clear that they are outward signs of planetary awakenings. Of course, the transformational message of each prophet will always be colored by the specific situation within which he operated. The challenge is to pluck the gem out from the historical sand around it.

This kind of talk about Moses is difficult. If it tastes like old history,

it's just one more chain around your head. Take these verses

as a prod to inner looking. It's the *light* of Moses that's our concern,

and that light doesn't pour down through time. It rushes up from

your chest. There's a sea-parting greatness that anchors our being,

and a hard-hearted Pharaoh in there too. Seek them out both,

these old adversaries. They'll play their parts till the end

of days just so you can learn where in the story you are.

Candles flicker, but the nature of of light ever steady.

Look at a candle, then *see as the flame sees*, every

thing is inside *your* light now. Become a seed, with all existence

coiled inside. This is called *joining the true believers*.

I F YOU ARE A TAILOR, STAY AWAY FROM THE FORGE,
OR LEARN FROM A SMITHY WHO'S MASTERED HIS CRAFT.

AND SMITHY, YOU SHOULD STEER CLEAR OF THE SEA,
OR SIT BY THE MAST AND KEEP A TIGHT GRIP.

BUT IF YOU LONG TO ROW THE RIVERS OF EDEN
AND LINGER AWHILE IN THE GARDEN OF LOVERS,

THEN GET TO KNOW JESUS, AND BECOME HIS TRUE FRIEND,

OR LOWER YOUR AIM.

T HE MIRACLE OF JESUS IS HIMSELF, NOT WHAT HE SAID OR DID
ABOUT THE FUTURE. FORGET THE FUTURE.
I'D WORSHIP SOMEONE WHO COULD DO THAT.

The man known to Christians as **Jesus**, to Muslims as **Issa**, and to his companions as **Ye'shua**, spoke the ancient Semitic language of *Aramaic*. In Aramaic, sacred words carry many shades of meaning, the better to reflect the ungraspable nature of divinity. When Jesus says **GOD**, his Aramaic is **ALAHA**. The understandings evoked by **ALAHA** are far more subtle and complex than those of **GOD**, which comes from the Germanic word for **GOOD**. According to Bible scholar Neil Douglas-Klotz, **ALAHA** would have been understood on the streets of Jerusalem as **O SACRED UNITY!** or **O ENCOMPASSING ONENESS** or **ALL** or **ULTIMATE POWER** or **ULTIMATE POTENTIAL** or **ONE WITH NO OPPOSITE**. In Hebrew tradition, the reluctance to freeze the ocean of Godhead into simple mental constructs is so strong that it is forbidden to say the Holy Name aloud, or even spell it out, reflecting Lao Tzu's insight *That which is called the Tao is not the Tao.*

O LORD OF LIFE-GIVING WATERS,
GRANT US OUR LIFE,
SAY THE WORD

·BE·

Soul of God

CHAPTER 1

One day a company of unbelievers came to visit the holy prophet, for they knew that he would feed them generously.

2　They were many, so Muhammad said to his companions, Do I not dwell within each of you? Therefore divide these guests up amongst you and minister to them, and it will be as if I am the host.

3　But when each of them had taken to himself a guest, there was one man left behind, a large sullen Turk, who sat on the steps of the mosque like thick dregs in a cup.

4　So Muhammad brought the fellow to his own home, and served him. But the gluttonous man devoured enough food for eighteen people, and drank the sweet goats-milk saved for others, so that the rest of the household were much angered at his greed.

5　Therefore when the man retired, a servant contrived to lock and seal the door behind him, so that when in dark of night he awakened with a great urgency to relieve himself, alas! the door was firm, so that even his knife could not free the bolt.

6　Thus imprisoned, he fell again into a disturbed sleep, and dreaming then that he was alone in a desolate place (for his soul was desolate) he pressed out from his bowels a great noisome load into the bed.

7　He soon awakened, and seeing his awful mess upon the bedclothes he groaned with shame, and thought to himself, "Surely my sleep is worse than my waking, for while my waking is a gluttony, my sleep is a pestilence."

8　Then in humiliation and self-loathing he waited for the sun to rise and the rattle of the door-opener, hoping only to make an escape before discovery.

9　The Blessed One came to the chamber at dawn, and lo! he made himself invisible that he might open the door and let the man escape without shame. Those absorbed in God like Muhammad may do this.

10　In due course a room-servant discovered the soiled bedclothes and showed them to Muhammad. He made no cruel remark, for he was a mercy to all beings, but smiled, and called for a washing-bucket. The others leapt forward to do the work, but the Prophet refused their assistance, saying, This is a secret duty, and straightaway began his onerous task.

11　Now, hurrying upon the road the Turkoman found that in his haste and confusion he had left a treasured amulet behind. Creeping back to recover the thing, he came upon the sight of the Messenger of God washing his awful linen.

12　Then a great confusing love flooded into his heart. All else was forgot, he rent his shirt and beat his head and flung himself before Muhammad. "You are Completeness," he moaned, "and I am a wretched nothing without the worth to look upon thee." And he shook and trembled with remorse.

13　Then Muhammad held him in his gentle arms, and caressed him like a child, and opened him like a flower, and made him whole.

14　The cloud weeps and the garden awakens; the infant wails and the mother's milk will suddenly flow.

15　And so the words of revelation say, LET THEM CRY A LOT.

Inscribed on the hilt of the Prophet's sword: *Forgive him who wrongs you; join him who cuts you off; do good to him who does evil to you, and speak the truth though it weigh against yourself.* The sword never saw use in battle; it was a symbol of *the Sword of Iman*—an alloy of implacable faith, certitude, and determination that helps a warrior of the spirit sever the knots of hatred and self-importance. When in the hands of a Buddha, it's called the *Diamond Vajra-sword.*

THE BLESSED ONE CAME TO THE
CHAMBER AT DAWN, AND LO!
HE MADE HIMSELF INVISIBLE THAT
HE MIGHT OPEN THE DOOR AND LET
THE MAN ESCAPE WITHOUT SHAME.

THOSE ABSORBED IN GOD
LIKE MUHAMMAD MAY DO THIS.

They point the Way
all of them, to the
Unchanging One.
So why do their words
turn in a hundred directions?
Their stories are
all over the place!
Are they talking
about the same thing?

A prince orders a great tent
to be made.
One craftsman winds the ropes.
Another sharpens pins.
Another sews panels. How
varied their activities,
how united their intentions,
and how single the task.

If there are 144,000 *Nabis*, was the Buddha one sent to the people of northern India? Some Buddhists believe he was an ordinary man who achieved supreme enlightenment; others put him in a celestial cosmology. Many Hindus claim him as an Avatar, another kind of *incarnation*. And what about earlier, even Paleolithic times? Are there traces of the soul-opening event coming even to those distant peoples?

The Messenger Comes, then Again and Again

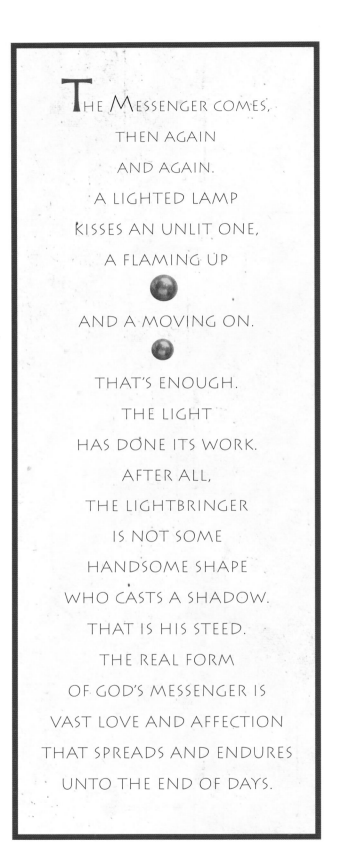

The Messenger comes,
then again
and again.
A lighted lamp
kisses an unlit one,
a flaming up
and a moving on.

That's enough.
The light
has done its work.
After all,
the lightbringer
is not some
handsome shape
who casts a shadow.
That is his steed.
The real form
of God's messenger is
vast love and affection
that spreads and endures
unto the end of days.

Candles flicker.
The nature
of light,
ever steady.

SOLOMON'S PRAYER

I've heard the only time God laughs is when men draw borders on the earth and declare, "This side is mine!"
If that's so, then the Eternal One must weep when we proclaim a piece of the earth as His—and then kill each
other to control it. This is a song about the Temple Mount in Jerusalem, and it offers what might be the only
lasting solution to this tragic turf war. I've kept Rumi's word *mosque* where you would expect *temple*. They orig-
inally meant the same thing. Can we hear them the same way again? A sage was once asked what his religion
was. "Whatever God's religion is, that's mine," was his answer. Sounds like the right congregation.

Solomon, he wished a place,
A place for to pray,
To the mystery,
The mystery of Yahweh.

He raised a dome of glory,
Far from stain or sin.
The place he called the Furthest Mosque,
There to worship in.

Built it not of earth and stone,
Fire, water, air.
They would but a prison make
For Solomon's vast prayers.

He built it of intention,
And wisdom clear as dawn.
Of mystic conversations,
Compassion for the wronged.

Every atom is alive,
Light moves from room to room.
Every part in harmony,
Carpet bows to broom.

Door and latch and all the rest
With ease together swing.
Like musicians in a band,
Or choirs of angels sing.

This sanctuary of the heart
Is real as your own face.
Real as every living breath,
As real as Our Lord's grace.

Mortal tongue cannot describe
A place so deep and high.
Nor bear the taste of God's embrace,
Why then do we try?

Temples made of earth shall fall,
Victims of time's toll.
But the mosque of Solomon
Is safe within your soul.

I Didn't Buy this Boat to Hang Around a Harbor

There's a flush of excitement. Somewhere deep in your chest a glacier has cracked and great hunks of ice calve into the sea. A letter arrives. It says *Come, come, and yet again, come!* We are starting on a journey, didn't you know, a love journey. There's a boat waiting, but it's not large, so we'll have to leave a lot behind, get used to traveling light. Rumi celebrates journeys, the outer reflection of inner movement, so the theme of casting off is always present. *Cut the rope and come to Me.* Rumi offers encouragement, advice, and hints on how to know if you're really ready.

If an oak could stretch out a foot,
would it wait around for the ax?
If the sun didn't roam all night,
how would the world turn rosy at dawn?
And if the sea did not rise so eagerly into
the clouds,
how could this green globe
be revived by rain?

Didn't Joseph have to know the length
of the road
before coming to happiness
and kingdom and victory?
Didn't the Prophet have to walk
a long thorny path before
he found safety, and
the love of a hundred lands?

And you?
When will you begin that long journey
into yourself?

You think I'm some luckless lover who
flees the dance? Look again. Did I pick
up this dagger to quit the battle?
Sure, I'm a crooked plank,
but not one that shrinks from the plane or
wanders off to the scrap pile.

I've waited centuries for this treasure to come
into view, there's no turning aside now.
So if I'm not excited by nightlife
and culture and sips of fine wine, don't get the
wrong idea. It's not a matter of taste.
I didn't buy this boat to hang around a harbor.

OU
LIVE ON THE SAME STREET FOR YEARS,
BUT WHEN NIGHT FALLS AND DREAMS ARISE,
YOU'RE IN A STRANGE NEW LAND
FILLED WITH MARVELOUS SCENES,
AND YOUR OWN HOME
IS FORGOTTEN.

JUST LIKE THAT,
LIKE A DREAM,
THIS VAGABOND WORLD
CONFUSES YOUR SIGHT.

NO WONDER
YOU CAN'T RECALL
YOUR REAL ADDRESS.

AND THOUGH YOUR SOUL
HAS WANDERED MANY REALMS,
YOU NO LONGER KNOW
YOUR DEEP BEGINNINGS
OR TASTE
YOUR GLORIED END.

Then comes a moment when we tire of our inherent isolation and begin seeking deeper connection. We perceive a pattern in the drama, a *quest* to which we are intuitively drawn. The problem is, *the one who sets out will never return.* This is why the quest is heroic even in unheroic times. It can only end in the end of everything we think of as ourselves. We may hear about "dying into a new life," but it doesn't help that much. Neither do stories about caterpillars and butterflies. A sign that you're ready for change is the nagging suspicion that you're only a visitor here, a stranger in a very strange land. For pilgrims, Rumi says good companions are essential, and someone who has already walked the path is best. Rumi sometimes points to Moses, sometimes Jesus, sometimes Muhammad.

If you knew yourself for even one moment,
if you could just glimpse your most beautiful face,
maybe you wouldn't slumber so deeply in that house of clay.

Why not move into your house of joy
and shine into every crevice!
For you are the secret Treasure-bearer, and always have been.

Didn't you know?

Thanks MAKARA, for holding so still while we poured rubber mold stuff all over your pretty face.

Some
Great Loving Intelligence

Has cast a veil over hearing and sight.

A little news slips through, but only what the Friend allows.
To the eye is given, sometimes,

A Glimpse of Vast Beauties

A glimpse of Vast Beauties, A Taste of Perfection,
The Tease of Amorous Glances,

no more. To the ear, given, sometimes,

Strains of Perfect Music, Glad Tidings, a Cry of Rapture,

but only enough to leave the heart impossibly lonely.

For every pain, a remedy has been created,

said the Prophet,

but no cure for this ache
until God opens wide your window.

You that seek a healing of this fine sorrow

SET YOUR GAZE OUTSIDE THE WALLS OF THE WORLD,
AS ONE ABOUT TO DIE TURNS IN A NEW DIRECTION.

I HAD SUCH A HOPELESS
DESIRE FOR
Y O U
TILL I SAW
HOW
YOUR LIGHT
YEARNED FOR ME TOO.
I PUSHED AND I PUSHED
TILL I SAW IT WAS YOU
WHO HAD
ALREADY
DRAWN ME
TO EVERY GOOD
THAT I KNEW.

Wanderer, stay hungry and
honor your exile.
Wherever we sprang from
in the first place,
that's where we're headed now.
Just don't plan on settling here.
See how you begin to get vague
as soon as you make plans?

From a dot of sperm to the strength of youth,
think how many chapters
you've passed through already.
Why stop now?
Who travels lightly escapes easily.
Try letting something go
just to see
what happens then.

FLEE FROM THE FOUR DIRECTIONS

FLEE FROM THE FOUR DIRECTIONS

FLEE FROM THE FOUR DIRECTIONS

Root and branch, inner and outer,
something enormously real
has taken hold of you now.
Now take hold of It!

   Don't you feel the soft touch, the
urge, the quickening in the heart?
Even the wind is in on this conspiracy,
flinging hints everywhere:

   When you're thirsty, keep moving.

And now a shout
from beyond the margins
of the world:
Flee from the four directions!
Here! Move this way!

When could a moth
ever ignore
such candle glow?

Fig 1. Selfish acts and crooked intentions will crowd around the heart.

dled • A true human being is not ruled by eating and sleeping • A true human being is the king in disguise • A true human being is a

Selfish acts and crooked intentions
    crowd around the heart.
Only a real warrior can
    tackle that army.

A warrior needs good weapons,
    and the best is companionship
with the lovers of mystery,
    the believers. Drop your spear and

join the caravan of those who set
    their course by a sun that never sets.
There's your holy war!
    No other decision meets more

resistance. Some part of you
    will twist and try to slide away,
for the sight of the good companions
    shames that scaly old ego.

Little snakes that have never
    seen a true human being
can grow into some
    very mean dragons!

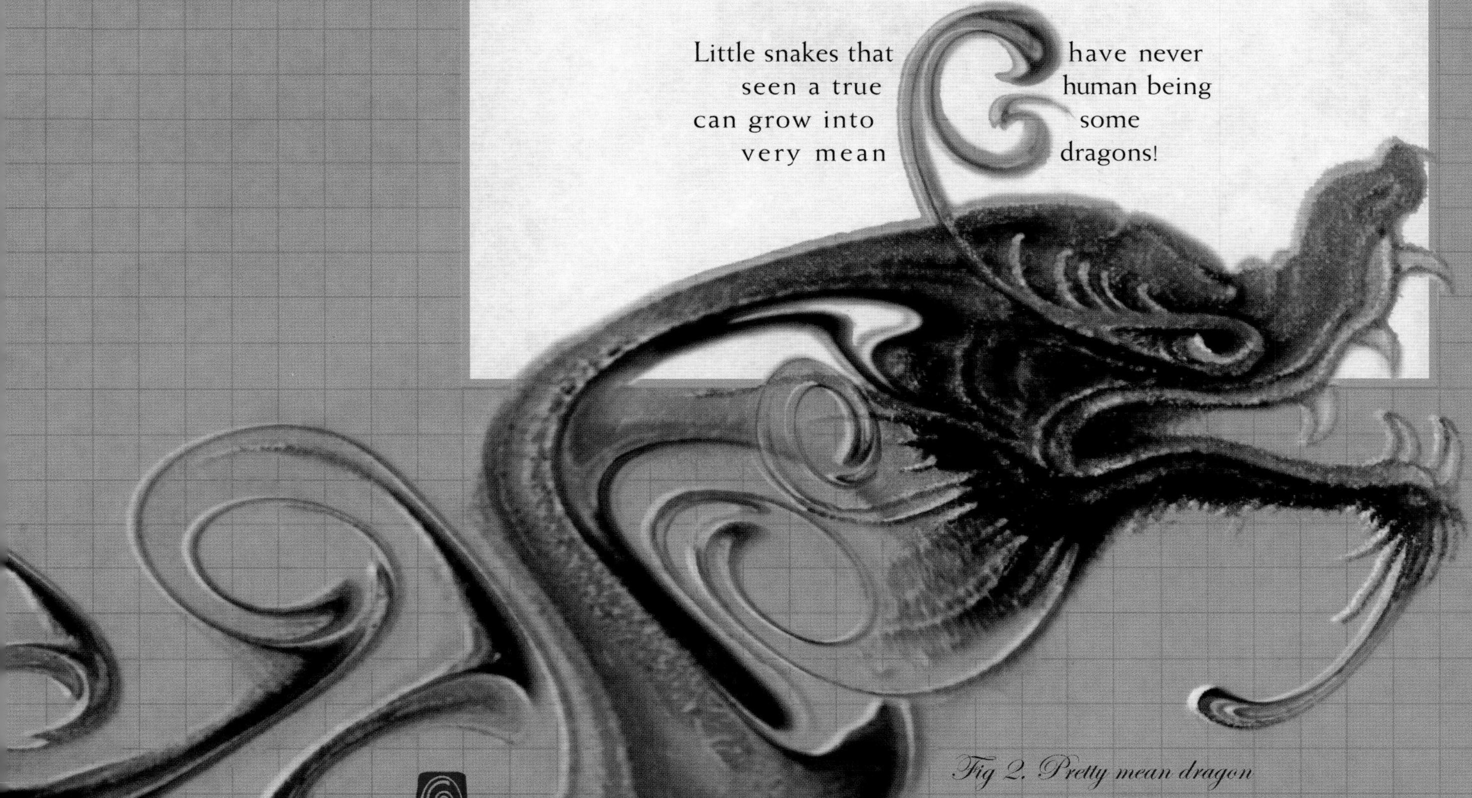

Fig 2. Pretty mean dragon

jewel in the dust • A true human being is not fashioned of elements • A true human being is a shoreless wide ocean • A true human being is a rain without clouds

A true human being sees truth face to face • A true human being is wise without reading • A true human being is without

You are the root of heaven, the
morning star, the bright moon,
the house of endless love.

My soul takes your image
into its heart as mirrors do,
my heart sinks like a comb
into wave after wave
of your silky hair.

So come with me into the lion's
thicket, and be not afraid.
Where we're going, no more
wounding, just mercy unfolding.
Only imagination can bar
this ancient loving way.

Come to the lions now,
tread warily,
keep silent heart:
this thicket is like tinder,
and your tongue is a match.

ZUNI LIFE PATH 1. SHOW UP, 2. PAY ATTENTION. 3. TELL THE TRUTH. 4. STAY OPEN TO RESULTS.

how

OW EXCELLENT THOSE
TRUSTWORTHY COMPANIONS WHO
FOLLOW THEIR HEART-SILENCE.

EVERYONE LOOKS IN SOME DIRECTION,
BUT THESE PRECIOUS ONES TURN
THEIR FACES TO THE DIRECTIONLESS.

EVERY BIRD IN THE AIR
HOLDS TO A COURSE AND A
PLACE IN THE WORLD.
      THESE DOVES SOAR IN THE VOID
      WHERE THE WHOLE WORLD RESTS.

WHATEVER WE ARE GIVEN IS ENOUGH,
ENOUGH, AND MORE THAN ENOUGH.
      DON'T YOU SEE?
WE NO LONGER SIT STITCHING THIS ROBE
TOGETHER. NOW WE STAY UP ALL NIGHT,
PULLING THE TRACERY APART.

The Wailing Wall in Jerusalem

A NIGHT FULL OF TALKING

There's no setting out right on journeys until you've set things right. Wings open only when the heart is open, and clear and honest. No shortcuts.

A night full of talking.
Around these cold hearts,
We've been walking.
This has been a long night
Full of talking,
    That hurts.

All the secrets,
All the worst secrets,
I've been holding back,
I've been holding back.
All the things I lack,
All the things I lack.
    That hurts.

    It's about loving,
    Everything's about loving.
    Or if you're not,
    All the rest can be forgot.

This night is long,
This night will pass.
And when it's through,
Oh, when it's through,
We got some work to do,
Hard, hard work to do.
    That hurts.

Now spirit sings,
Oh spirit sings,
But you gotta do some hard things,
You gotta do some hard things,
For that swan to spread her wings,
Those beautiful wings.

    Oh the swan gonna spread her wings,
    Them beautiful wings.
    Did you ever hear
    How spirit sings?
    How spirit sings?
    How spirit sings?

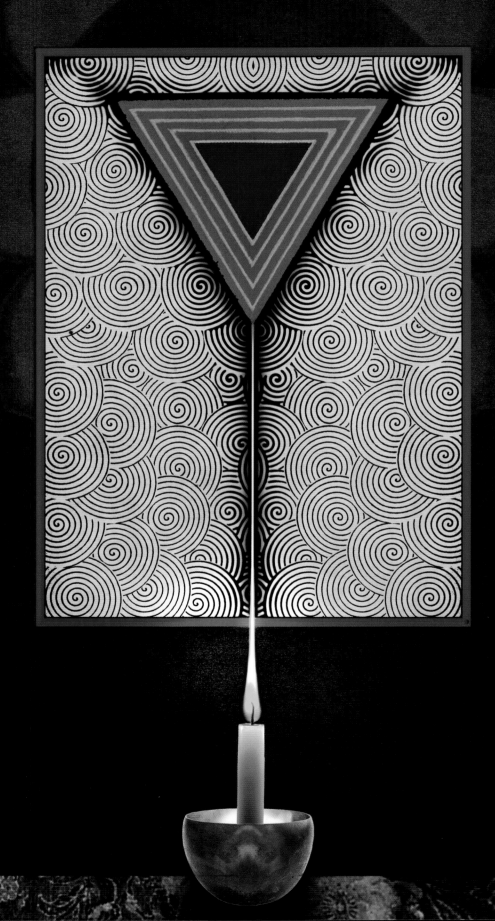

You are the original Original; I am
your faithful mirror. That tall cypress
and its shadow, might as well be
        you and me.
And if you are a rose, I am rose-shadow.
All beauties have their followers,
        but roses have a way of fading,
and I have a way of holding on too tight.
        I turn all thorn then,
but you come back again and make
my thorniness fragrant
                and pink and petaled.
        So here is the cup of my heart
and a toast. *To us! Every moment to us!*
Why do I reach out anywhere else?
Only your touch works out in the end.

        You are my candle,

                I am your bowl.

The long procession of prophets moves through the ages. *Sound the cymbal, strike the harp, the King has come!* But what about the Queen? Is there a *silver chain*? The Marys, Rabia, Zulaikha, Fatimah, Kuan-Yin, Green Tara, Hildegarde, Sarada Devi, White Buffalo Woman, Ananda Mayi-Ma, on and on? But fishing for parallel construction seems a little forced. The divine feminine arrays herself more naturally as a web. And even if there's a long list, illumined women are more invisible. Dying into bliss is not done for a place in history. Good lovers slip into their chambers, draw the curtain, and disappear. Maybe women are better at it. Rumi honors the feminine by saturating his poetry with female sweetness.

Rumi opens to all the shifting moods of the Divine. Sometimes it manifests as the nurturing intimacy of a mother, some-times as a male energy so vigorously brilliant as to turn us all into blushing brides. Sufis recognize, like other sacred tradi-tions, that the polarity observed everywhere in the workings of the world is reflected in the human condition. Bawa once remarked there are only two races, *male and female*. As men and women, we embody two universal principles, and getting along might be easier if we honored the differences as well as the commonalities. A wonderful illustration of this is found in Iroquois culture. Men are seen as having a greater need to be in charge, so daily governance is given to a circle of chiefs. Women are bearers of a different wisdom: as mothers they deal with the world in a more intimate way. Since they've raised the men from birth, and know who shared and who was a bully, the clan mothers *pick the chiefs*. And if a chief goes off course, the good ladies unseat him in a ceremony marvelously called "Pulling-the-Horns." Imagine Congress running like this. There are two kinds of power honored here. Immediate action, and something slow, deep, and healing: soft roots growing through rock. Are women the natural guardians of root strength? I'll go with those who think so. Men have it, but it has to be teased out.

A WOMAN IS A MYSTERY
THAT CAN GUIDE THE WISE AND OPEN MAN.

THERE'S ANOTHER KIND OF MALE
WHO KEEPS A CAGED ANIMAL INSIDE

HIMSELF. HE'S GOT TO DOMINATE.
NO TENDERNESS OR BLESSINGS THERE.

BUT IT'S TENDER KINDNESS THAT
MAKES US HUMAN,
ANGER AND HOT DESIRE,
SOMETHING LESS.

PERHAPS SHE REALLY IS A LIGHT
FROM GOD,
AND NOT THAT
SOFT AND
ROUNDED FORM
YOU SEE.

MAYBE SHE IS
THE BREATH
OF CREATIVITY,

MAYBE
SHE WASN'T
CREATED
AT ALL!

The oldest book of all, the I Ching, says, *It is the Creative that begets things, but they are brought to birth by the Receptive.* When the last drum is stilled, woman mystery is in the silence that opens, the empty space through which all the hosannas unfurl. Male knows; female is. Male is specific, female pervasive. Male is honor, female contentment. Male speaks, the female is silence. It is into this perfumed silence and emptiness that all Rumi poems eventually turn, gliding out of the known and the bounded on great silent wings. "The Glorious One within me," Rumi said at the end of his life, "has never uttered a word." This is supposed to be the chapter on woman mystery. Actually, woman mystery drifts like the fragrance of orchids through every page.

The day
    When mountains move
        has come.
Though I say this,
        Nobody believes me.

Mountains sleep
Only for a little while
That once
        Rose up in flames.

But even if
    You have forgotten—
        People! Just believe!

        All the women who slept…
            Awake now
                And move!

—Akiko Yosano   (Trans. by Kenneth Rexroth and Ikuko Atsumi)

I AM THROUGH WITH EVERYTHING BUT YOU.
I AM DYING INTO YOUR MYSTERY, AND
DYING, I AM NOW NO OTHER THAN THAT MYSTERY.
I OPEN TO YOUR MAJESTY AS AN ORCHARD
WELCOMES RAIN, AND TWENTY TIMES THAT.
I AM REJOICING, I AM A BEGGAR
GIVEN GOLD WITH NO GIVER IN SIGHT.
NOT UNITED, NOT SEPARATED, I TRY
WHISPERING PERFECTION, BUT NO
SOUND COMES. YOU ARE BEYOND
DESCRIPTION, BEYOND EVEN
REASON TO BE.

WE ARE THE FISHES IN YOUR SEA,
WE ARE YOUR GESTURES
AND YOUR PLEASURES.

BUT O, MY LOVE, YOU ARE NOT
APPROACHED BY THOUGHTS
LIKE THESE.

LOVE
IS NOT APPROACHED
BY THOUGHT AT ALL.

Saliha

Sufis say that the soul draws in grace like an infant nursing on its mother's breast. The Original Islam that Rumi reveals is grounded in this mother's-milk intimacy with the Beloved. The first words of Muhammad's revelation are *Bismillah ir Rahman ir Raheem*, IN THE NAME OF GOD, THE INFINITELY COMPASSIONATE, THE ETERNALLY MERCIFUL. In Arabic grammar, God–*Allah*–is masculine, but God's preeminent qualities of compassion and mercy are not only feminine, but derived from the word *womb*. The Prophet honored Mary in a special way. Returning to Mecca after exile, his first act was to cleanse the house of Abraham–the *Kaaba*–of the graven idols that had collected there. But he ordered that an image of Mary remain. The script in this Madonna picture is a *Bismillah* greeting from a letter sent by the Prophet.

...BUT THIS GOLD IS ONLY CAUGHT BY THOSE
WHO MAKE THEMSELVES AN
EMPTY SPACE BEFORE IT.

I AM A CUP CAUGHT
IN THE HAND OF LOVE. IF YOU
DON'T BELIEVE ME, LOOK IN MY EYES.

OR BETTER STILL, LISTEN
TO MY HEART,
BEATING LIKE CRAZY.

BUT WATCH OUT!
THIS LOVE IS NOT THE PALE
AND SLENDER TYPE.

SHE IS DRINKING IN
ALL THE LOVERS
RIGHT NOW!

Who is this emerging from the primeval ocean? The multicultural eye may discern the powerful, dark-skinned, feminine aspect of the divine called Kali. She is said to rule over this present, last exciting age, when everything hidden and dangerous in the human psyche is revealed, to be cleansed away by her truth-or-conse-quences presence. Is Kali the *She* doing the "drinking down" in this poem? Unlikely. Rumi was attuned to *the principle* she embodies, but he remained a devoted Muslim. He slipped into the unchart-ed territory outside all belief-systems, but would return to the guidance of one set of wisdom revelations, one set of sym-bols. This picture, like much of this book, is taking liberties in order to make the point of our planet's underlying unities. Desperate times call for desperate measures.

BE
TRUTHFUL NOW,

SEE YOURSELF AS YOU PLAINLY ARE.

YOU'VE GOT A HIDDEN WOUND,

AND THIS IS NO TIME FOR POSING.

WHEN

INWARD TENDERNESS

FINDS THAT SECRET HURT,

THE PAIN ITSELF WILL CRACK THE ROCK

AND, AH! LET THE SOUL EMERGE.

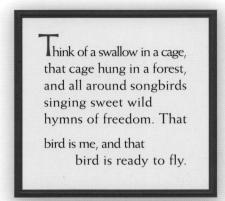

Think of a swallow in a cage,
that cage hung in a forest,
and all around songbirds
singing sweet wild
hymns of freedom. That

bird is me, and that
bird is ready to fly.

When inward-looking tenderness appears to heal and awaken, we may recognize what Lao Tzu calls THE Valley of the Dark Woman.

LET BEAUTY NOW BE

The Vedas report that a true lover of God is artistic, musical, even an accomplished cook. I love the idea that aesthetic richness is innate in the human condition and needs only a lift of the spirit to be activated. Graceful life-skills as the afterglow of grace. Sometimes beauty allows a glimpse of the Soul. Rumi says, *Let music loosen our deafness to spirit.* There's a yielding quality here. The masculine looks for comfort in ideas; the feminine would rather the heart be released in song.

Some mornings we wake up on empty
To a day that's got nothing but need,
So we reach for a cup of strong coffee,
Or maybe the Good Book to read.

The words in the gospels are golden,
But they come from so high and so far,
That sometimes it's true the best thing to do,
Is pick up a good old guitar.

> *Let the beauty we love come and fill us.*
> *Let the beauty all around get us through.*
> *Let the beauty inside be our compass.*
> *Let beauty now be what we do, what we do.*

Cause all hearts do long for a beauty,
A secret that's hid everywhere,
And a soft sweet old tune can remind us it shines
In the midst of the deepest despair.

There are hundreds of ways joy can find us,
Like the hundreds of ways children play.
There's hundreds of ways to kneel down on the ground,
Hundreds of ways we can pray.

> *Let the beauty we love come and fill us.*
> *Let the beauty all around get us through.*
> *Let the beauty inside be our compass.*
> *Let beauty now be what we do, what we do.*

We are witness today to the emergence of an ancient spiritual vitality into modern affairs. Gary Snyder calls it the *River of Sanity*, an underground current running through all history. It comes from the deepest wellsprings of our humanity, and it moves us into harmony with the natural world and with ourselves. It does not contradict scientific thought, but offers a profoundly wider way of engaging reality. It is caught rather than taught. It balances masculine and feminine. Rumi is a Rivervoice. This book is part of an emerging art dedicated to illuminating the River. It scans the entire spread of human achievement for points of light, ancient or modern, sacred or scientific. Working with source material from Lascaux to internet downloads, it seeks energetic links and revelatory unions. A Koranic blessing meets the Dead Sea scrolls. Old-time Persian quatrain meets old-time slide guitar.

Praised as a sculptor once, Michelangelo objected.. *Not I,* he said. *Sometimes I look at a block of stone and see a figure imprisoned inside. All I do is remove what doesn't belong.* That's good direction for this process too: keep alert, follow Instructions, try and stay out of the way.

ΛND IF EVERY WAY IS

CLOSED BEFORE YOU,

THE SECRET ONE

WILL SHOW A

SECRET PATH

NO OTHER EYES

HAVE SEEN.

Ordinary human life starts with a few complex hydrocarbons and a Plan, then turns into a huge, often tragic tangle. When the Twin Towers fell, we all shared for a few impossibly astonished and alert minutes an unfiltered taste of the tragic. A curtain lifted on a tougher world-view than the one we knew, and we shifted a little closer perhaps, to the truth of things. This life is a lift into light and a fall into ruin, both.

The Hebrew kings donned sackcloth to atone for the sins of their people, but the modern ruler prefers to maintain a happy-face. Things may go a bit off at times, but there's no ill that American know-how and might can't put right. However, as the Book of Changes observes, *It is only when we have the courage to face ourselves exactly as we are that a light will appear by which we can extricate ourselves from the present circumstance.*

What are present circumstances? Andrew Harvey outlines the situation like so: *We are in a massive psychic depression. This depression is everywhere and eats away at every resolve we take, at every passion and every attempt at health. It is a massive worldwide depression and its cause is a fundamental loss of our identity, our memory of our divine origin.*

One of Rumi's strengths is his ease with jams-ups. Comic or messy, they spice up the story and create opportunities for soul-growth. Sometimes it's only sitting in the pit that we *get it*, and a change of heart can take place. How to learn in the ashes? Rumi suggests growth and healing happen if we can drop our resistance to how things really are, and just see and allow exactly what the moment is bringing. It's like the Zen story of the monk hanging from a cliff. Above a hungry tiger prowls; below, jagged rocks. What does he do? He sees a wild strawberry growing out of a crack beside him and tastes it. Not bad! *Acceptance can change everything.* Not optimism, not pessimism, just allowing a situation to take form, trusting in something deeper. Accepting yourself is another kind of acceptance that can turn lead into gold. Something stirs inside hardness; old patterns get unstuck, a new kind of love is felt. Call it surrender. When we get off our tiptoes and stop reaching for future perfection, stop wishing that things were other than they are, we might find something a whole lot better.

O Maker
of Mysteries,
Who makes every
stranger a friend,
Who has given
the rose to the thorn
as a robe of honor,
sift our dust again!
Make our nothing
something.

FRIEND, LEAVE ASIDE ALL THE OTHERS
AND SPEAK OF YOURSELF.

SAY WHAT YOU POSSESS AND
WHAT YOU HAVE FOUND,
AND WHAT PEARLS YOU HAVE DRAWN
FROM THE DEEP.

WHEN THE SENSES
FALL INTO DARKNESS,
WILL YOUR HEART
BE A TRUSTWORTHY FLAME?

WHEN DUST FILLS YOUR EYES,
WILL YOUR GRAVE STILL BE BRIGHT?

WHEN HANDS AND FEET FAIL,
WILL YOU RISE THEN
ON GREAT SILENT WINGS?

Every midwife knows
not until a mother's womb softens from the pain of labor
will a way unfold and the infant find that opening to be born.
Oh friend! There is treasure in your heart,
it is heavy with child.
Listen. All the awakened ones, like trusted midwives,
are saying, welcome this pain,

It opens the dark passage of Grace.

THERE'S A **GRAND INTELLIGENCE** THAT VISITS TRIALS UPON YOU AND FROM EVERY DIRECTION TOO.

ALL JUST MANEUVERS DRAWING YOU BACK TO NAMELESS CENTER.

IF YOU'VE SET YOUR HEART
    A LITTLE TOO
        KEENLY

ON SOME
    WONDERFUL SOMETHING,
        WATCH OUT!

SEVERITY
    FROM GOD-KNOWS-WHERE
        WILL SNATCH IT FROM YOU.

 MY LOVE! DO NOT
    CLING

TO ANY
    LITTLE
        SOMETHING.

Seek wisdom even unto China. —a saying of the Prophet (May God sanctify his secret).

When Rumi says Do not cling to any little *something*, it covers a lot of ground. The word has to be understood in a way that speaks to the liberation of the soul. If you can touch it, wave flags about it, go to war over it, it's *something*. Our ideas about God can be a particularly stubborn *something*. Rumi is suggesting that actual embrace of the sacred demands a kind of awareness free of stickiness and entrapment. *When the heart is released from clinging*, the Buddha preached, *then mind does not land anywhere.* In one of the great sermons on the subject, he once assembled his disciples, then merely held up a flower. In the Sufi tradition, Presence manifests in 99 ways. One of them is AL-DHARR, or "Magnificent Severity." Clarity that cuts like a sword. *Ka-chunk, Hallelujah.* This is demanding territory.

LUMINOUS BEING OF SHINING LAKEWATERS,
AND LUMINOUS STILL
IN CLAY SUN-CRACKED AND HARDENED,
WHEN THE WATERS HAVE GONE.

O LUMINOUS BEING IN THE RICHES OF HARVEST
AND LUMINOUS STILL IN
THE FAMINE THAT FOLLOWS
WHEN HARVESTS ALL FAIL.

O LUMINOUS BEING
SUDDENLY BRIGHT IN NIGHT LIGHTNING,
YOU ARE LUMINOUS STILL IN THE DARKNESS THAT SETTLES
WHEN LIGHTNING IS SPENT.

— MANSUR AL HALAJ

There is a blindness Sufis call The Veil of Light caused by self-righteousness and religiosity that can be more dangerous than the Veil of Darkness created by vice. How exhilarating to be sooo right! Sometimes the only thing that can break through the Veil of Light is finding yourself up to here in trouble. In the ecology of the soul, life's devastations have important work to do, like the creepy-crawlies in soil that break garbage down into humus. Recognizing that there may be blessings in bad times encourages our roots to find nourishment in the darkness, even as we are being pruned down to nothing on the surface. *To live among the ruins and sanctify the wastes*, is how poet David Federman puts it. The passage of devastation is well-known to recovery groups, and one of the reasons for the unexpectedly honest strength one finds in AA meetings.

是 THIS function of religion does not fortify the separate self but utterly shatters it: not consolation but devastation, not entrenchment but emptiness, not complacency but explosion, not comfort but revolution—not a bolstering of consciousness but a radical transformation at the deepest seat of consciousness itself. This transformation is not a matter of belief but of the death of the believer, not a matter of finding solace but of finding infinity. The self is not made content; the self is made toast.

—Ken Wilber

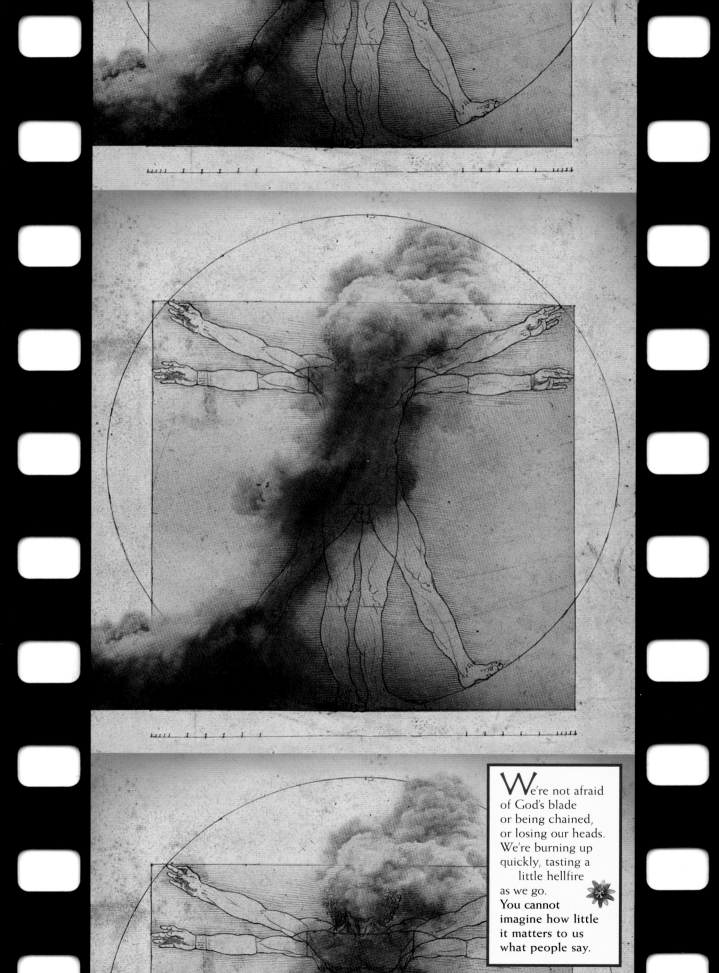

We're not afraid
of God's blade
or being chained,
or losing our heads.
We're burning up
quickly, tasting a
little hellfire
as we go.
You cannot
imagine how little
it matters to us
what people say.

FEEL ME THE FIRMNESS

At some point we begin to miss the presence of something we never knew existed. A great sorrow wells up from a place hidden behind the numbness of the heart. In a song like this, Rumi is going down there to gather companions, and he doesn't mind. There's a wonderful hope in these kind of tears.

O my friend, my one Beloved,
Our closeness is like this it's true,
Anywhere you put your perfect foot,
Feel me the firmness beneath You.
I am the firmness beneath You.
Feel me the firmness beneath You.

Lord, I pray to somehow be
Wherever your sweet foot comes down.
Perhaps by chance before You step,
Your glance will fall upon my ground.
All blessings are in that look found,
Salvation in that look abounds.

How is it with such deep devotion,
And with my love forever new,
I see Your world in all its splendor,
But O Sweet Lord, I can't see you.
O God, my God, I can't see You.
O God, my God, what shall I do?

O COMPANION,
LOOK AROUND.

YOU
ARE NOT
SOME
LOCAL
APPEARANCE.

YOU

ARE THE
BRIGHT
BLUE SKY

AND
THE DEEP
GREEN SEA.

YOU

ARE A
VAST
OCEAN,
THE
DROWNING
PLACE OF A
THOUSAND
LITTLE 'I'S.

Life on planet earth provides the reasons to hassle one another. Prophets provide the damage control: *Do unto others as you would have them do unto you.* At first blush the commandment seems like a call to resist the way things are—nature being a sort of continuous Darwinian riot, with guidelines more like *Do unto the other before the other does unto you.* But Sufi experience does not agree. It suggests that the Golden Rule puts us in step with the way things *really are.* Unfortunately, this way that things really are is so totally *out there,* so counter-intuitive, that it's usually just alluded to poetically, or shown by example. But for the scientific mind, here's one possible outline of *How Things Really Are*:

- *The external world is not* at all *how it seems.*
- *Neither are you.*
- *Beneath the convincing separateness of things is a vast, indescribable, loving Unity.*
- *That Unity is your true identity.*

These words are like a shard of sun-bleached bone on the beach. Evidence of *something,* but what? Seagull? Whale? The matter in question is nothing less than the root of religion and science both, something *prior* to conduct codes and cloud chambers. It gets marginalized by orthodoxy as its "mystical branch," but, root or branch, it's where the sap is flowing. It's what Christ urges us toward when he suggests we die to our selves and be *born again.* It's why Sufis pray *There is Nothing other than God; God Alone is Real,* and Buddhists chant *Form is Emptiness, Emptiness is Form.* It's Yaqui shaman Don Juan sweeping his surroundings with a grand gesture and declaring, *How can I know who I am, when I AM ALL THIS?*

The station of I AM ALL THIS regards all dogmas with a certain equanimity because it has *awakened* from the realm of dogmas. Like Galileo casting aside Church doctrine and peering into his telescope, it is a seeing into Reality directly, not descriptively. Explained, *I-AM-ALL-THIS* is as debatable as science fiction, inscrutable as mod-

ern physics. Experienced, it's plain as the nose on your face. (Plain, that is, with a shift in focus from what is far to what is near.) In that wonderful, flawed parable, Neo *wakes up* from the Matrix. Meher Baba writes on his chalkboard, *You and I are not we but One.* Jesus declares, *The kingdom of heaven is within you.* Muhammad's call to prayer drifts across the oasis, *Only God is Real.* But perhaps Rumi is close to the truth when he says, *There's no saying this right... but I'll try again.*

A beautiful argument can open your mind to new truths, convince you, say, that the earth orbits the sun. A belief system change can be a life-altering experience. But Rumi is not exactly inviting us to a change in belief systems.

> *We know another way of knowing*
> *that leads to wonder beyond wonder.*
> *Turn this way for illumination, not*
> *for winning arguments.*
> *Here, logic and proof are a blind man's staff.*
> *When this luminosity dawns, look! you're free.*

Rumi is rather inviting us to a *change in awareness* as substantial as waking from a dream. In our ordinary life we direct our attention wheresoever we wish: to clouds outside a window, to the window, or to words in a book. *Clouds* or *window* or *book* are all apparently *out there. We,* on the other hand, are *in here,* inside our bodies, mysteriously aware, the Looker, perhaps. But what if we shift *attention* from cloud/window/book to our own *open field of consciousness* where these things are so nicely displayed? From *here,* it should be obvious, this book, far from being 18 inches distant from the Looker, is fully engulfed or displayed *inside* the Looker. The Looker *which is itself consciousness.* (Which is what turns **black squiggles** into concepts.) In fact, says Rumi, *out there* couldn't possibly be more *in here.* The master snaps his fingers, the spell is broken, and—Oh!—*the world* is no longer at remove from our awareness of it, from consciousness, from "me." *Me is now a vast, open, grace-filled spaciousness.*

THIS RESTLESS DANCING WORLD,
FLAG IN THE WIND.

SPIRIT, SEE THE WIND.

NOW LOOK
FOR THE GREAT STILLNESS
THAT HOLDS
THE WIND.

EVERYTHING ELSE

IS GONE,

GONE,

ALREADY GONE!

All this may sound like word-play, and is, but it's also what Buddhists call *Highest Perfect Wisdom*, and the Upanishads, *Knowing That by which all else is known*. It's a figure-ground shift that can feel as natural as a mother's kiss, or knock you off your feet on the road to Damascus. To paraphrase the Bible, *Once we saw through a glass darkly, now we see face to face. Once I knew in part, now I know fully, even as I am fully known.* Rumi's gift is to infuse this great knowing with the warmth of personal relationship.

The consequences of this knowing are huge. *Doing to others as you would have them do to you.* is a very different ball game when the *Other* his become non-separate from yourself. Living in a world—*a reality*—experienced without any significant Other calls for some pretty radical recalibrations. "On the whole," says Annie Dillard, *"I do not find Christians, outside of the catacombs, sufficiently sensible of conditions. Does anyone have the foggiest idea what sort of power we so blithely invoke? Or, as I suspect, does no one believe a word of it? The churches are children playing on the floor with their chemistry sets, mixing up a batch of TNT to kill a Sunday morning. It is madness to wear ladies' straw hats and velvet hats to church; we should all be wearing crash helmets. Ushers should issue life preservers and signal flares; they should lash us to our pews. For the sleeping god may wake someday and take offense, or the waking god may draw us out to where we can never return."*

It's the fragrance of this direct experience, *I-AM-ALL-THIS*, that keeps religion alive. It is as true for Evangelical Christians as Zen Masters or Muslim dervishes. Theological belief systems still rise and fall on their own merits. But amid the clamor of competing doctrines the purity of *I-AM-ALL-THIS* is a True North. It always agrees. It doesn't answer questions so much as pull them out by the roots. It's the song we all can sing.

But there's still no saying this right.

This is a light abounding in full gladness, like coming upon a light in thick darkness, like receiving treasury in poverty. So easy, so free are you, that the weight of the world and the aggravations of the mind are burdens no longer; your existence is delivered from all limitations. You have become open, light and transparent. You gain an illuminating insight into the deepest nature of things, which appear to you as so many gossamer patterns having no graspable reality! Here is the original face of your being. Here is the straight passage, open & unobstructed. Here is where you surrender all. This is where you gain peace, ease, non-doing & inexpressible delight. All sutras and scriptures are nothing more than communications of this fact. All the sages, ancient and modern, have exhausted their ingenuity and imaginations to no other purpose than to point • the • way • to • **this**.

Kanji calligraphy "THIS" by tea master Kokosai. Quote by Shih Shuan

What's the catch? If freeing the soul was as simple as figuring out an Escher drawing, most of us would be liberated. The problems we have awakening from a real life dream are instructive. Everyone has struggled to shake off a nightmare, or lingered in some sexy fantasy. Either way, it was our fascination with the things in the dream that kept the goings-on so real, and the waking up difficult. Letting go of fear and desire baggage is called purifying the heart, and it's the core work of this Path. Those enamored of dreaming need not apply.

I saw a bush
and I saw it was burning.
    I heard a voice
and it called me **Beloved**.

    Am I Moses?
My soul surely has wandered
    the wilderness,
tasted God's manna and,
    wept with affliction.

Come, my soul, my secret,
    my innermost flame!
If you are my Moses,
    this body is your staff.
If you are my Jesus,
    here I am, the sparrow
you pressed from mud.

    O formless
Maker of forms,
    please tell me now
what form are You?

Background topology: computer simulation of DNA

hOW FAR IS IT?
HOW FAR IS THE LIGHT OF THE MOON
FROM THE MOON?

HOW FAR
IS THE TASTE OF CANDY
FROM THE LIP?

THE BEAUTY
YOU CRAVED IN
THINGS WAS
ALWAYS MY
FACE SEEN
THROUGH A VEIL.
TURN AROUND.
SEE NOW WHERE
BEAUTY COMES
FROM.

The secret of seeing, is, then, the pearl of great price. If I thought he could teach me to find it and keep it forever, I would stagger barefoot across a hundred deserts after any lunatic at all. But although the pearl may be found, it may not be sought. The literature of illumination reveals this above all: although it comes to those who wait for it, it is always, even to the most practiced and adept, a gift and a total surprise. I return from one walk knowing where the killdeer nests in the field by the creek and the hour the laurel blooms. I return from the same walk a day later scarcely knowing my own name. Litanies hum in my ears; my tongue flaps in my mouth, Ailinon, alleluia! I cannot cause light; the most I can do is try to put myself in the path of its beam. It is possible, in deep space, to sail on solar wind. Light, be it particle or wave, has force: you rig a giant sail and go. The secret of seeing is to sail on solar wind. Hone and spread your spirit till you yourself are a sail, whetted, translucent, broadside to the merest puff.

—Annie Dillard

TRY ANOTHER WAY OF LOOKING

TRY YOU LOOKING

AND THE WHOLE UNIVERSE

SEEING.

These dust clouds in the constellation Aquarius are worth reflecting on. The tails at the top are called "cometary knots." What's interesting is that ers is about twice the size of our entire solar system. *Something wonderful* says cosmologist Brian Swimme, *when, staring at these puffs, one suddenly* thing. Something on a whole other *order* happens, say the Light- these same star- one suddenly grasps that the clouds, AND the con- are, for heaven's sake, *one incomprehensible unity, one song, world without end, amen.*

gossamer puffs of gas with each of these little stream- *happens to one's consciousness.* *grasps the scale of the whole* bringers, when, staring at sciousness doing the staring

OUTER PASSES,
ESSENCE ABIDES.
WHY KNEEL BEFORE
SOME JUG OF CLAY?
LET IT BE,
START SEEKING WATER.

TAKE THE PEARL
AND LEAVE THE SHELL

BEHIND.

Loneliness seeks company.
Separation gropes for form.
But this is the hour of union when
emptiness opens its arms saying,
Come, I am the root of firmness
and ecstasy both.

You've been in love with reflection.
Now embrace their origin. Come,
let nothing stand between us. Let
us be naked face to face seeing.
        Water spills from a rock.
The rock disappears.

COME, MY LOVE, YOU'LL HAVE TO LOOK DEEPER
THAN THAT FOR THE DOOR TO THE CENTER—
    IT'S HERE.
I AM THE HEART OF YOUR HEART.
    IF YOU NEED TO RIPEN, FIND
SOMEONE WHO'S SLIPPED
FROM THE NOOSE OF TIME.
    THEIR EVERY ATOM IS HELP.
AND IF YOU'RE THINKING
YOU ARE OTHER THAN ME, YOU
DON'T KNOW YOURSELF, AND
    THAT'S A HARD
ROAD TO SUFFER.
COME, MY LOVE, WE'RE SO
PART OF EACH OTHER.
    DON'T PEEL AWAY
FROM YOUR WHOLE
ANY LONGER.

            HERE...

CLING TO THIS COMPLETENESS.

ONCE MORE WE RETURN TO THE STORY.

...BUT WHEN
        DID WE EVER LEAVE IT?
IF WE SINK BACK TO IGNORANCE,
        WE'RE GUESTS IN HIS PRISON.
IF WE MOVE TOWARD MINDFULNESS,
        WE'RE WALKING IN HIS GARDEN.
IF WE ENTER SLEEPWALKING,
                IT'S STILL HIS DREAM.
IF WE WEEP,
        WE'RE TASTING HIS TEARS.
IF WE LAUGH,
        IT'S A FLASH OF HIS SUMMER LIGHTNING.
RISE UP WITH A SWORD, THERE!
        A GLINT OF HIS STRENGTH.
ARRIVE WITH PEACE AND FORGIVENESS,
        WE'RE A SIP OF HIS LOVE.
SO NOW WHAT ARE WE?
        IN THIS WHOLE TANGLED WORLD, WHAT
IS THERE OTHER THAN THE FRIEND?
        LOOK!

EVERYTHING,
ONLY ONE BRUSH STROKE.

SAY I AM YOU

This song is an anthem to the oceanic awareness of non-duality. The melody to Say I Am You *comes from a beautiful old Gospel ballad called* Heavenly Shore. *Nine out of ten mystics agree, if reality is only known through consciousness, then for all practical purposes, we may assume there is nothing other than consciousness!*

I am the dust that
floats in bright sunlight.
I am the sun, too,
burning so bright.

Say to the dust, stay,
And to the sun, keep
Moving in circles,
Wake us to light.

I am the mist of
Sweet early morning,
And the soft breathing
When evening is born.

I am the wind in
Swaying green branches,
Taking my chances
As surf pounding shore.

I am the tall mast,
I am the deep keel,
Rudder and bowsprit,
Helmsman and wheel.

Now I am also
The perilous reef,
The snares and delusions
That bring them to grief.

First I the silence,
Then I the choice,
To take form as this song,
Now I the voice.

I am the candle,
And the moth flying,
flirting with dying,
As it goes round.

I the rose blooming,
And at the same time,
Nightingale lost in
Fragrance sublime.

All orders of Being,
Galaxies turning,
Intelligence burning
In evolution.

I am the lifting,
The falling away,
Living and dying,
Night and the day.

In all things created,
Known and forgotten,
I am what is,
And what is not.

Master of masters,
One within all,
You who so know me,
Answer this call:

Say now the secret,
Say the word true.
Say what the heart knows,
Say I am You.

Thomas Edison suffered most of his life from near deafness. At the end of his years he hired a pianist to come to his studio and play the world's great waltzes as loudly as possible. Listening, sensing some wonderful thing he had spent a life not knowing, finally in frustration–and perhaps some abandon–he dropped to his hands and knees and bit into the wood of the piano, the better to let the sound vibrations run into teeth and bone and inner ear. Getting something from these pages is similar. There is a waltz neither words nor picture nor song can convey in completeness. To hear it, Rumi must be bitten into, chewed, and finally, contemplated in silence.

O Please Come Back to Me

REMEMBRANCE

The musicians play softly now; the scent of jasmine is drifting in the breeze; our hearts fill with indescribable longing. *The Garden is near.*

Near, but where? In the Gospels, Paul famously advises garden-seekers to *pray without ceasing*. It's a vague instruction appearing in all the great traditions. Ramakrishna clarifies the idea further, saying it's like the mood of a nursemaid whose thoughts are constantly dwelling on her own child in another village: what seems far is felt as near. The heart of the Sufi Way is to cultivate this shift in focus through remembrance of the Beloved. Remembrance is sometimes evoked by chanting or bodily movement, but its most refined form is a silent flow of attention that rides every breath, *the Zikr (or Remembrance) of the heart.* Hints of this work are scattered throughout Rumi:

> *Let me sit close to the Love Place, near as breath is to body.*

But no specific instructions. His poetry is less a manual than a mystery tour to loosen our embrace of the familiar world and turn us, blinking and lovestruck, in another direction.

The practice of Silent Remembrance balances on a contradiction. Somehow, like the reed in the song, we have been pulled from our original home, but nothing we can possibly *do* will return us to the the riverbank. *Doing is the problem.* Doing reinforces the idea of a stiff ego-self as "doer." Coming Home is more a tender undoing. Christians call it Grace.

But even in undoing, a bit of *doing*—a practice—can help. The noble Prophet said,

> *For everything there is a polish which takes away rust, and the polish of the heart is Remembrance.*

Let us polish ourselves to such a thinness that glimmers of light shine through. Polish to exhaustion, that weary of doing, the only thing left is to chuck the whole works. Including ourselves.

WIND,
AND A TREE GENTLY
WAVING.

REMEMBRANCE,
AND THE HEART-LEAVES
TREMBLE.

Remembrance, as taught by the Sufi Boddhisattva Bawa Muhaiyaddeen, is rooted in a simple and detached observation of your own breathing. Sit comfortably; let breath become deep and generous. Refined energies are moving, as well as oxygen and carbon dioxide. Become the witness of it all. *Within breath, the visible and invisible worlds meet.*

Awareness of breath is then joined with awareness of the great prophetic message, the magnetic field that charges all of Rumi's poetry:

THERE IS NO REALITY BUT GOD / THERE IS ONLY GOD
or THE "I" IS AN ILLUSION / GOD ALONE IS REAL

These are Bawa's renderings of the testament of faith called the First Word, or *Kalima*. I once asked if it is best recited in the more mystical Arabic, LA ILLAHA / IL ALLAHU. *It could be in Arabic or in English,* he said, *but Remembrance isn't words at all.* Remembrance is the Breath of Love and its only association is the *Beloved,* the ocean of light called *Alaha* by Jesus, and *The Great Mystery* by native peoples. Remembrance is a heart-current activated by longing and gratitude and praise.

God has said,
The images that come with human language do not correspond to Me,
but those who love words must use them to come near.
Just remember, it's like saying of the king, "He is not a weaver."
Is that praise?

Remembrance is a secret possibility that ebbs and flows in every breath. Seeking it, we can disappear into it, a steep narrow pathway that opens to breathtaking vistas.

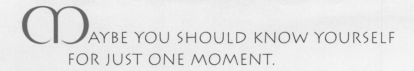MAYBE YOU SHOULD KNOW YOURSELF
FOR JUST ONE MOMENT.

MAYBE YOU SHOULD GLIMPSE
YOUR MOST BEAUTIFUL FACE.

MAYBE YOU SHOULD SLEEP LESS DEEPLY
IN YOUR HOUSE OF CLAY.

MAYBE YOU SHOULD MOVE INTO THE HOUSE OF JOY,
AND SHINE IN EVERY CREVICE.

MAYBE YOU ARE THE BEARER
OF HIDDEN TREASURE.

MAYBE YOU ALWAYS HAVE BEEN.

YOU MAY LEARN
THE ART OF BIRD CALLS,
BUT WILL YOU KNOW WHAT THEY ARE SAYING?

IF YOU TRILL LIKE A NIGHTINGALE,
WILL YOU WEEP WITH ITS LOVE FOR THE ROSE?

DON'T THINK
YOU'RE GOING TO UNDERSTAND THESE MESSAGES
FROM THE UNSEEN JUST BY READING,
ANY MORE THAN THE DEAF CAN LEARN TO SING
BY WATCHING A SINGER'S LIPS!

THE I IS AN ILLUSION

GOD ALONE IS REAL

THE OUTFLOWING MOON BREATH

Once attention has settled onto breathing, let THE I IS AN ILLUSION (*La Illaha*) join with the outbreath. A subtle wind is visualized moving upward through the body, the heart, and the restless mind, then exhaled. Feel this breath carrying everything negative and unwanted along with it: illnesses, self-delusions, obsessions, fears and angers, destructive desires—all the debris mind gathers to fabricate ego. Give them all up as unsubstantial, gossamer, as smoke and shadow.

THE INFLOWING SUN BREATH

Let each inhalation become a *breath of love*, and mingled with it is the profound understanding GOD ALONE IS REAL (*Il Allahu*). Breath passes through the nose up to the gnostic eye in your forehead, first spreading light through the brain, then flowing down to the inner heart and merging with the soul. Truth-yearning arises in the heart, drawing great luminous Presence to itself. Finally it flows everywhere within, "illuminating all the universes." *Now Two ceases and One begins.*

STRIPPED AND NAKED,

A MAN RACES TO THE RIVER,

A CLOUD OF HORNETS

IN HOT PURSUIT. THEY'RE

HIS OWN TEN THOUSAND

SWARMING DESIRES AND

THAT COOL DEEP WATER IS

THE PRECIOUS REMEMBERING:

GOD, GOD,

THERE IS NO REALITY BUT GOD,

THERE IS ONLY GOD.

IF HIS HEAD COMES UP

THOSE HORNETS ARE

ALL OVER HIM AGAIN.

FRIENDS,

TRY BREATHING WATER,

BECOME RIVER.

HORNETS ALWAYS LOSE INTEREST.

One morning I stepped out of Bawa's room onto the second floor porch facing Overbrook Avenue. Inside, it was just little problems and daily affairs. I sat on the wrought-iron couch. *This endless talk.* But what about the lightning bolt of grace? Why was it always striking some time in the future? Like revelation, I suddenly saw that whenever the Holy Now burst open, it would actually be *right here and now.* A mood of fierce elation swept over me. Enough! I would dive this moment into the practice of remembrance till it was done.

Breathe in, breathe out, settle in. Somewhere in the house lunch was served, but lunch was no longer my concern. In and out. Keep back straight, ignore aches. Shadows slowly lengthened. In, out...

Finally, the pure *dryness* of it all was ovewhelming. Resolve crumbled into resignation. *But as will collapsed,* every maple on the street lit up, each leaf clear and luminous. All sounds in the neighborhood shimmered as consciousness. Ah, how elegant, how perfect. And how, I wondered, do I capture this beauty as an artist? Instantly the rapture dimmed. The door to Bawa's room opened, and my old friend Ione appeared, somewhat puzzled. She handed me a flat coin-shaped candy wafer like I used to get at the movies as a kid. "Message from Bawa," she said. "He said to tell you, *'Ten cents.'*"

TRY BREATHING WATER, BECOME RIVER.

O PLEASE COME BACK TO ME

How can it not be so: the Beloved is nearer than the throbing of our own hearts, and sweet union our natural condition. Rumi opens to the mysterious Friendship, laments its mysterious passing, seeks the mysterious remembrance.

What in that candle's light that opened me?
What in that starry night would consume me?
Was done so wondrous right and so quickly.
What in that candle's light that opened me?

There's shadow in my sunlight, please let me see.
Nothing can help me now but Your beauty!
In gratitude and wonder I'll always be.
Nothing can help me now but Your beauty!

O please come back to me, my only friend,
O please come back to me.
O please come back to me, my heart to mend,
Your love has no beginning and has no end.

There was a dawn as soft as rosy wine.
The sun it seemed to rise inside my mind.
The sky so rosy red, so still, so fine,
In stillness then your soul it spoke to mine.

O please come back to me, my only friend,
O please come back to me.
O please come back to me, ourselves to blend,
Your love has no beginning and has no end.

I drank the holy waters inside your spring,
The spring became a river, why should I cling?
I felt the current take me, I had to sing.
I sang the song of All and Everything.

Let these words fly through time
to someone coming.

You know who you are.

This love
has nibbled on your ear,
whispering secrets that don't
make sense to anyone else.

Where is this poem going?

It's late, our master's
eyes have closed in sleep,
the musicians play softly.

But stay with me, friends, stay.
Guard these words like gold.
You are shining stars,
every one of you.

Now
go and find you
Your Sun!

...AND EVEN IF THIS WORLD BURNS UP
HIDDEN HARPS WILL STILL PLAY HERE.